How Does It Work?

COMMUNICATIONS TECHNOLOGY

**John Hilvert and
Linda Bruce**

MACMILLAN

LIBRARY

First published in 2005 by
MACMILLAN EDUCATION AUSTRALIA PTY LTD
627 Chapel Street, South Yarra 3141

Visit our website at www.macmillan.com.au

Associated companies and representatives throughout the world.

National Library of Australia
Cataloguing-in-Publication data

Bruce, Linda.
Communications technology.

  Includes index.
  For upper primary school students.
  ISBN 0 7329 9744 5.

  1. Communication – Juvenile literature. I. Title. (Series:
  How does it work? (South Yarra, Vic.).

621.38

Edited by Anna Fern
Text and cover design by Modern Art Production Group
Illustrations by Andrew Louey
Photo research by Legend Images

Printed in China

Acknowledgements
The author and publishers are grateful to the following for permission to reproduce copyright material:

Cover photo: Man using computer, courtesy of Photos.com.

AAP, pp. 4, 21; Ask Jeeves, Inc, p. 29; Canon, p. 25; Rob Cruse Photography, pp. 6, 14, 23; Digital Vision, p. 17;
Istockphoto.com , pp. 8, 10, 27; By permission from Microsoft Corporation ©, p. 26; NOAA, p. 18;
Photolibrary.com, p. 24; Photos.com, pp. 1, 22; Productbank, p. 11; Science Photo Library, /Simon Fraser, p. 5,
/Cordelia Molloy, pp. 12, 20, /Mehau Kulyk, p. 13, /Lawrence Lawry, p. 19, /Volker Steger, p. 30.

While every care has been taken to trace and acknowledge copyright, the publisher tenders their apologies for
any accidental infringement where copyright has proved untraceable. Where the attempt has been unsuccessful,
the publisher welcomes information that would redress the situation.

Contents

Glossary words

When a word is printed in **bold**, you can look up its meaning in the Glossary on page 31.

What is technology?

Technology helps us to do things. Technology is also about how things work. Since ancient times, people have been interested in how things work and how they can improve technology to meet their needs. They use their experience, knowledge and ideas to invent new ways of doing things.

The *How Does It Work?* series features the design and technology of machines that are part of our daily lives. This includes:

- the purpose of the technology and its design
- where it is used
- how it is used
- materials it is made from
- how it works
- future developments.

Technology has changed the way we live in many ways. It will keep on bringing change, as people constantly invent new ways of doing things using new materials.

People living in remote areas rely on the mail service, phone and Internet to communicate with the outside world.

Communications technology

To talk to each other and swap information is a basic human need. Since ancient times, people have invented ways to communicate further and faster. Tribal people cupped their hands to their mouths to make their voices carry further and used smoke signals. They imitated animal sounds in order to communicate without alerting strangers, and left signs for others to follow.

In the past, being a long way away meant being difficult to contact. Today, communications technology enables us to use devices such as telephones to quickly contact people in most places on the planet. The Internet enables us to swap information between millions of people. We can even use satellite communications technology to send messages to people and machines on the Moon, Mars and beyond.

This book takes an inside look at different kinds of communications technology. It also previews some amazing new inventions in communications technology that you might use in the future.

Satellite telephones enable people in remote places to communicate instantly with the rest of the world.

Landline telephones

A landline telephone enables people to talk to each other over long distances and connect to the Internet. Modern telephone lines can also carry cable TV and computer games.

Where used?

Telephones are used everywhere, including homes, businesses and other public places. All landline telephones need to be connected to a telephone line.

How used?

Users hold the handset and press a telephone number on the keypad. The signal travels to its destination and rings the telephone there. The person receiving the call picks up the handset, speaks into it and listens.

Materials

Telephones are mainly made from light, cheap, durable plastic. Smaller internal parts are made from metal, which easily conducts electrical signals. Telephone calls travel by radio and along **cables** made from metal or glass.

handset

stretchable cord

keypad

Landline telephones are easy to use.

How do telephones work?

A telephone changes the caller's voice into electrical signals which can be sent to other locations. Every telephone has an **exchange** number, which determines the path the signal takes. A call travels to its local exchange and from there to a main exchange. A telephone switch is the brains of an exchange. It sends calls from one telephone to another, connecting two or more **circuits** together, according to the dialled telephone number. At the receiving end, the telephone changes the electrical signals back into sound.

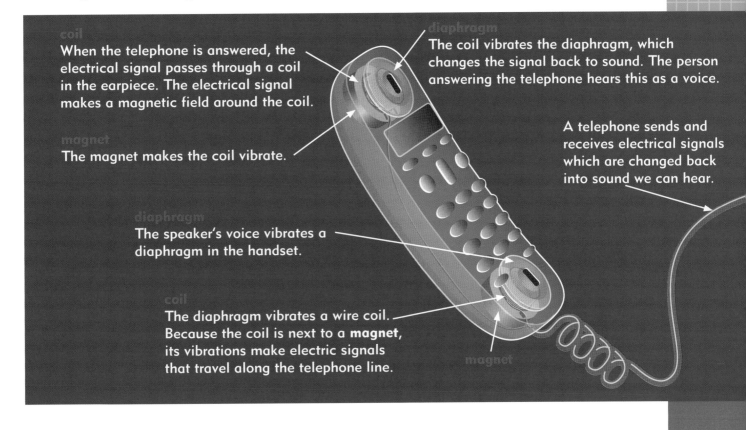

coil

When the telephone is answered, the electrical signal passes through a coil in the earpiece. The electrical signal makes a magnetic field around the coil.

diaphragm

The coil vibrates the diaphragm, which changes the signal back to sound. The person answering the telephone hears this as a voice.

magnet

The magnet makes the coil vibrate.

A telephone sends and receives electrical signals which are changed back into sound we can hear.

diaphragm

The speaker's voice vibrates a diaphragm in the handset.

coil

The diaphragm vibrates a wire coil. Because the coil is next to a **magnet**, its vibrations make electric signals that travel along the telephone line.

magnet

What's next?

In the future, you may be able to make a phone call using a throat phone on the outside of your neck. Rather than changing the vibrations that the sound of a voice makes through the air, the throat phone changes vibrations from the vocal chords in the neck into electrical signals. Throat phones would be useful in a noisy environment, such as in traffic or at a party.

Mobile telephones

A mobile telephone uses radio signals to connect to the phone exchange.

Where used?

Mobile phone calls can be made and received anywhere there are radio towers for mobile phones. Most populated areas have these towers. Mobile phones may also be designed to communicate over more remote distances using **satellites** when out of range of **transmission** towers.

How used?

When a person wishes to make a call, they press a phone number on the keypad and send the call. The person receiving the call hears their mobile phone ring and accepts the call by pressing a button. They then listen for a voice and answer it. Many mobile phones include an address book, calendar, alarm clock, games and camera.

Materials

Mobile phones are mainly made from plastic. This material is chosen because it does not break easily when dropped, it is easy to mould into shape and it looks stylish. Inside the phone, small **microprocessors** made of **silicon** link to keypads to manage dialling and receiving calls.

Mobile phones are a popular way to stay in touch.

How do mobile phones work?

Mobile phones change the speaker's voice to radio waves and send these waves to the nearest mobile relay tower. From the tower, the signal is forwarded to its destination. Every few minutes, mobile telephones beam a radio signal to alert the exchange where they are and to which mobile relay tower calls to that mobile need to be directed.

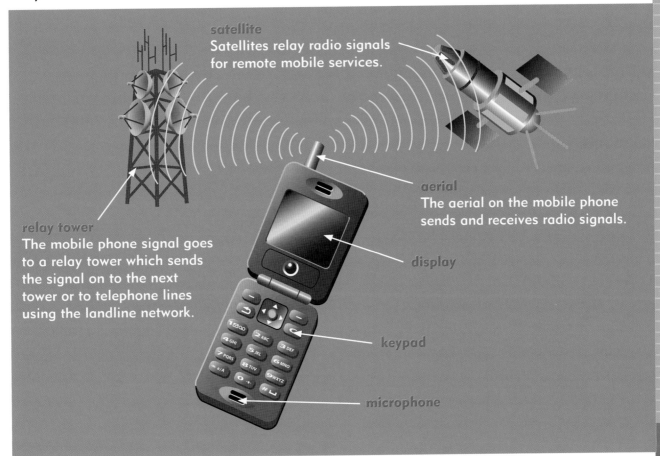

satellite
Satellites relay radio signals for remote mobile services.

aerial
The aerial on the mobile phone sends and receives radio signals.

relay tower
The mobile phone signal goes to a relay tower which sends the signal on to the next tower or to telephone lines using the landline network.

display

keypad

microphone

What's next?

In the future, we may use mobile finger phones. A tiny telephone in a wristband receives the call. To listen, the person receiving the call places a finger in one ear. The sound vibration travels from the wristband, up the bones of the hand and into the ear. Bone conducts sound better than air, so the caller can be clearly heard. The person with the finger phone speaks into the microphone on their wristband.

SMS text messages

SMS (short message service) delivers brief written messages over mobile-phone networks, at a lower cost than voice phone calls.

Where used?

SMS is available all over the world, wherever mobile phones can be used. It is particularly popular with young people.

How used?

The message sender uses the mobile-phone keypad to type words onto a screen. They send the message to the mobile telephone number of the person receiving the message. The telephone receiving the message displays a message symbol on its screen and the message can be viewed and stored. Senders can string several messages together to form a longer SMS. SMS users can subscribe to services to receive the latest news and sport information.

Materials

Text messages are displayed on screens made from plastic and **liquid crystal**. Light plastic keypads are used to send and manage messages.

Some mobile phone users prefer SMS because it is cheap and fun to send and receive text.

How does SMS work?

The short message service is a 'store and forward' service. Messages are not sent directly to a person. They are stored at a network SMS centre. This enables messages to be delivered to the receiver even if their phone is not switched on or if they are out of range at the time the message was sent. Messages are sent to the person's phone only when it is switched on and within range of a mobile relay tower.

Sending a text message
The sender types a message on their phone keypad and presses the send button.

The message signal goes to the nearest mobile relay tower and from there to a main telephone exchange.

The message is stored on a computer at the SMS centre.

Receiving a text message
When the receiver switches on their phone, the message goes to it.

The receiver's phone beeps to alert its owner that it has received a message.

message display

keypad

send button

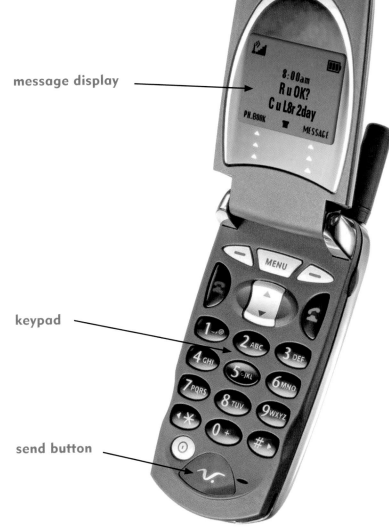

What's next?

At the moment, messages have a 160-character limit. In the future, mobile-phone users will be able to send longer messages. Keypad typing will be replaced by voice-dictated messages.

Radio services

Radio **transmitters** use **electromagnetic** waves to send data and sound to radio **receivers**. Because radio waves travel through air instead of cables, they are called 'wireless' services.

Where used?

Radio broadcasts can be received anywhere there are transmission towers. Radio receivers can be small and portable, so that people can receive broadcasts wherever they go.

How used?

Radio was an early form of mass entertainment which began around 1920. One radio signal sent out by a radio transmission tower can be received by many radio receivers. Radio is now used with many other devices, such as televisions, mobile phones, radio-controlled toys and space machines.

Materials

Radio sets are made from plastic. The **circuitry** and radio-wave reception parts are made of metal.

? Radio waves

Radio waves can be compared to waves on the ocean. AM radio stations send out waves at a particular height (called amplitude). FM stations send out waves with different amounts of space between them (called frequency).

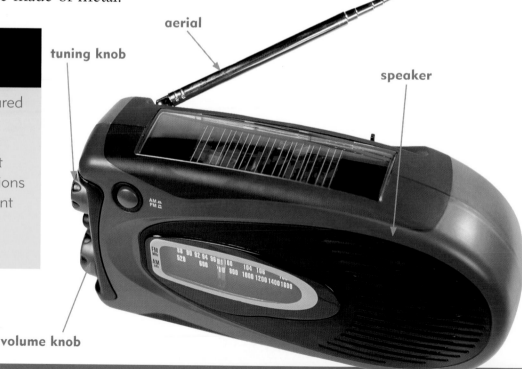

aerial

tuning knob

speaker

volume knob

How do radio transmitters and receivers work?

Radio transmitters transform sound into radio waves. A radio wave is a form of electrical energy that travels through space. Radio receivers detect radio waves, and change them back into sound that we can hear.

The radio station
The transmitter changes sound going to a microphone into radio waves.

Radio waves
Radio waves ripple out from the transmitter like waves in water. A radio wave is an electromagnetic wave which is sent out by an antenna.

Radio receiver
By tuning a radio receiver to a specific amplitude or frequency, you can pick up a specific signal, such as a particular radio station.

Radio waves travel out from transmitters at the speed of light (299 792 kilometres per second).

gamma rays | X-rays | ultraviolet rays | visible light | infra-red light | microwaves | radio waves

The radio waves used in these things are all a type of electromagnetic radiation.

What's next?

In the future, wireless radio services will replace many telephone cables such as those used in homes and in **network** links between computers.

Televisions

Television (TV) is a way of sending sound and video to audiences.

Where used?

People watch TV at home for entertainment and news. Portable TVs can also be used when camping or attending sporting events.

How used?

The home TV has an aerial to receive signals from TV transmitters. Home televisions are powered by **mains electricity**. Portable TVs are powered by batteries. Television receivers are designed to be easy to use. Remote controls or buttons on the set are used to select stations and adjust volume and image.

Materials

Television sets are made from heavy-duty plastic, metal and glass. These materials are chosen because they are easy to maintain and safe to use.

Most children learn to change a TV program before they can read or write.

How do televisions work?

The TV station transmits the picture by scanning it and sending one line at a time. These small bits of video information are changed into radio waves. Television sets change these radio waves back to pictures and sound.

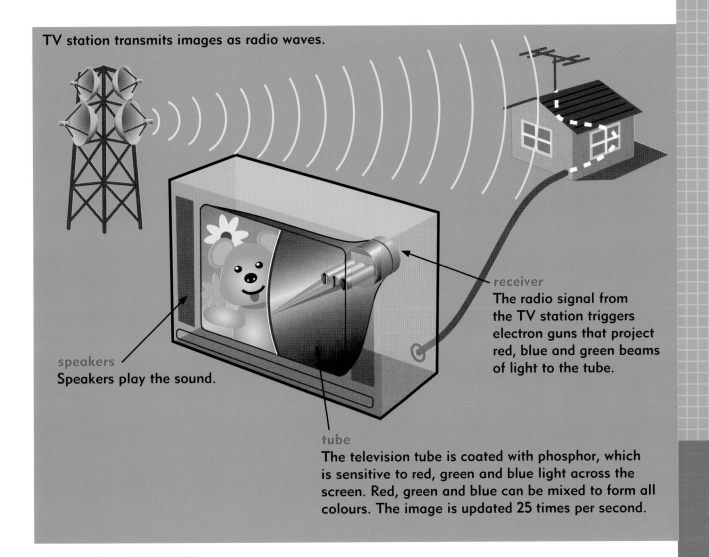

TV station transmits images as radio waves.

speakers
Speakers play the sound.

receiver
The radio signal from the TV station triggers electron guns that project red, blue and green beams of light to the tube.

tube
The television tube is coated with phosphor, which is sensitive to red, green and blue light across the screen. Red, green and blue can be mixed to form all colours. The image is updated 25 times per second.

What's next?

In the future, small TVs may be built into devices that look like sunglasses. The wearer will see the image on a screen in front of their eyes, and hear the sound through ear buds placed in their ears.

Satellites

Communications satellites are space machines that transmit and receive communications to and from Earth. Satellites enable communication across large distances and to remote parts of the world.

Where used?

Space shuttles and rockets carry communications satellites into space and place them in **orbit**, about 35 800 kilometres above the Earth's equator. Satellites travel at the same speed as the Earth spins (about 1690 kilometres per hour), so they appear fixed in the sky. This is called geostationary orbit.

How used?

Satellites, such as the Australian AUSSAT, are used to relay telephone conversations and live television broadcasts from one continent to another. Satellites also relay radio signals between tracking stations on Earth and spacecraft such as radio telescopes, probes, landers and rovers. Satellites also detect radio signals from stars, galaxies and other activity in space.

Materials

Satellites are made from strong, light metal **alloys**. **Solar panels** made of silicon produce electricity to run the equipment on the satellite. These materials are chosen because they are light, strong and last a long time.

Communications satellites can track and communicate with moving objects such as aircraft, ships and submarines.

How do communications satellites work?

Satellites have on-board computers, a power source such as solar panels, and small rocket boosters to ensure their transmitters point the right way to send and receive signals. Most satellites can be controlled from the ground.

solar panels

radio transmitter and receiver
Radio and television waves travel in a straight line from their source, such as TV stations. Communications satellites reflect them back to Earth at an angle, broadcasting them around the world.

rocket thrusters
Rocket thrusters keep the satellite on its correct orbit and pointed the correct way to send and receive signals.

batteries
The electricity needed to run the satellite is generated by the solar panels and stored in batteries.

What's next?

In the future, satellites that can be folded will be sent into space. After they have been launched by a rocket, the satellites will unfold and inflate. These satellites will be much lighter, which will make them much cheaper to launch.

Transcontinental cables

Transcontinental cables carry international communications across and between continents.

Where used?

Transcontinental cables are buried under the ground or laid on the sea floor. Major undersea communications cables run between the west coast of the United States of America and Australia, Japan and South-East Asia. They also run from the east coast of the United States of America to Britain and western Europe. The two cables that are used most run between the United States of America and Canada, and the United States of America and Mexico.

How used?

Transcontinental cables carry telephone conversations, live television broadcasts, Internet and other data communications.

Materials

The cables have a core made of metal such as steel, with glass fibres, called optical fibres, woven around the core. These materials are chosen because they move information in the form of electrical signals and light quickly. They are also strong enough to withstand pressure and wear from lying at the bottom of the sea.

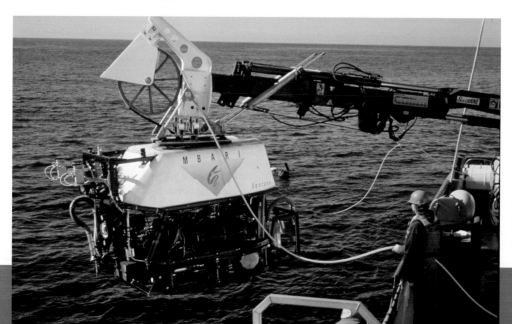

These workers are laying transcontinental cables under the sea.

How transcontinental cables work

Transcontinental cables were originally built with copper wires. Since 1988, optical fibre cables have been used because they can carry a much higher load of signals at far higher speeds. These signals may include coded voice communications or computer data.

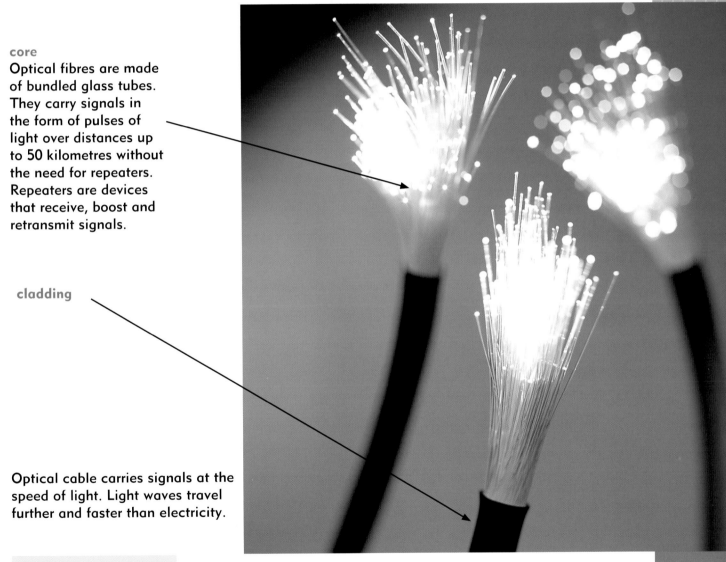

core
Optical fibres are made of bundled glass tubes. They carry signals in the form of pulses of light over distances up to 50 kilometres without the need for repeaters. Repeaters are devices that receive, boost and retransmit signals.

cladding

Optical cable carries signals at the speed of light. Light waves travel further and faster than electricity.

What's next?

The cost of laying cables has become cheaper, so that they can be replaced with even more powerful cables every five to seven years. This will promote a huge increase in global communications in the future.

Global positioning systems

A global positioning system (GPS) can locate a receiver's precise position on Earth by using the transmissions from communications satellites.

Where used?

GPS services are used all over the world. They are especially useful in helping people to navigate their way in the bush or at sea.

How used?

GPSs are used in many ways. Some are used to help people locate where they are by broadcasting and receiving signals to determine location, height and movement. Scientists can use GPS to track the movements of animals, such as white pointer sharks and fruit bats. A GPS can also be used to signal for emergency help.

Materials

GPS units are mainly made from metal and plastic. These materials are chosen because they are reliable, compact, safe and easy to use, and weather resistant.

A GPS can tell you where you are on a map, distance travelled and your estimated time of arrival.

How do global positioning systems work?

The GPS sends a radio signal to the satellite. A computer on the satellite works out latitude, longitude and height anywhere on or above the Earth's surface.

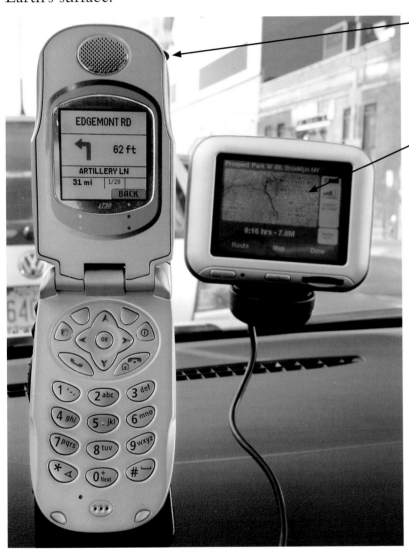

GPS receiver
The GPS sends a radio signal to a GPS satellite. A computer on the satellite sends the information back to the GPS receiver on Earth.

screen
The GPS screen displays the location. It is accurate to about 10 to 20 metres. Another kind of receiver called a 'differential GPS' is accurate to within 1 metre. In this system, the signal goes from the satellite to a receiver station at a fixed location on Earth, and then to the small GPS receiver unit.

What's next?

In the future, mobile phones will have built-in GPS devices to show the person receiving a call the approximate location of the person making the call. This will make it easier to find a person if they are injured in a remote location.

Personal computers

A personal computer is a tool that enables people to create and store information.

Where used?

Personal computers are used in homes and offices. Smaller notebook computers and hand-held personal digital assistants may be carried and used when people are travelling.

How used?

Individuals use personal computers to prepare written documents, organise information (such as business accounts), play games, and even to create artwork and music. Computers are also used to communicate on the Internet. Most computers have a graphical user interface (GUI) desktop and a mouse and keyboard to send commands and control the computer.

Materials

The case of the computer is mainly made from metal and plastic with a glass screen for its display. These materials are light, strong and easy to maintain. Inside the computer, some of the circuitry is on chips made from silicon.

Computers are vital to modern communications.

22

How do computers work?

Each computer has programs, or software, on it. When a user commands a program to start, the computer uses its central processing unit (CPU) to carry out the command. The CPU is a series of circuits that fit on a fingernail-sized chip called a microprocessor.

CD drive
Programs and information stored on floppy disc or CD can be loaded onto the computer.

modem
The modem connects the computer to the Internet.

scanner

speakers

printer

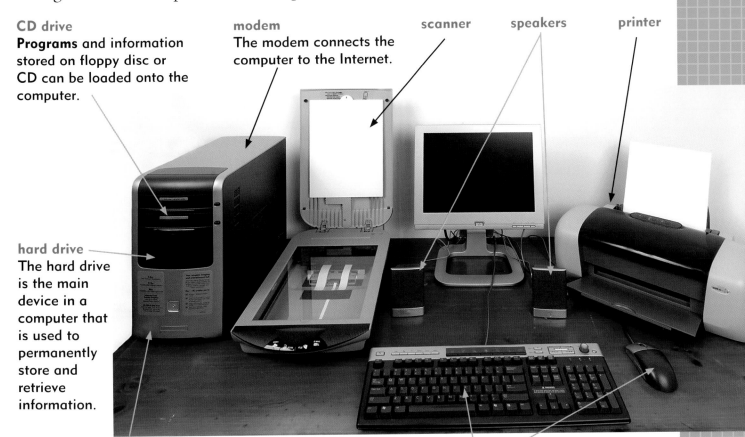

hard drive
The hard drive is the main device in a computer that is used to permanently store and retrieve information.

CPU
The CPU (central processing unit) translates the program commands into binary code. In binary code, 1 represents 'electricity on' and 0 represents 'electricity off'. The computer translates this code into images on screen and the sound we hear.

controls
The person using the computer sends commands to the computer by pressing keys or moving a mouse, joystick, steering wheel, brake, plane controls or data glove.

What's next?

In the future, computers will become even smaller and smarter. They may become part of personal gear such as clothes, head-wear, belts and wallets.

Fax machines

A facsimile machine (or fax) makes a copy of a document or illustration and sends this over the telephone line to another fax machine.

Where used?

Fax machines can be used in offices and homes that are connected to a telephone line.

How used?

A document is placed on the feed tray of the fax machine. When the start button is pushed, the machine rolls one page through at a time, making a **digital** copy of the page. It sends the digital copy over the telephone line. The fax machine at the other end of the phone line receives the signal and prints a copy of the document or picture sent.

Materials

Fax machines are mainly made from solid plastic with rollers made from rubber. These materials are light, strong and easy to shape. Some fax paper is made from special coated heat-sensitive paper. The printing ink is made from oil.

To send a fax means you are sending a copy of a document to another person over the telephone line.

24

How do fax machines work?

The sending fax machine scans and changes images into electrical signals which it sends along the telephone line. The receiving fax machine changes the signal back into an image made up of fine black-and-white dots which are printed out one line at a time.

1. The sender places the page to be faxed in the feed tray and presses the telephone number on the number pad.

2. Inside the fax machine, an image sensor maps the images on the page into a grid of tiny squares. Each square registers as black or white.

3. The pattern is converted into electrical impluses—on for black or off for white. These impulses are changed to sounds which are sent down the telephone line.

4. The receiver's fax machine interprets the signals and builds up the message line by line.

What's next?

In the future, faxes will be able to be sent in colour. Fax machines will also be able to receive complicated instructions from within the fax message, such as a command to print 100 copies of page two of the fax.

The Internet

The Internet is a vast number of private, public, business and educational computer networks which exchange information.

Where used?

The Internet is accessed all over the world. In 2004 there were more than 600 million users in the world.

How used?

People log onto the Internet by using a computer connected to a telephone line, or a radio connection. They use the Internet to send email and other digital information such as documents, pictures, movies, music and software. People can also visit web pages and chat rooms on the Internet.

Materials

The Internet uses computers made from plastic and metal, with **silicon chips.** The telephone lines are made from metal and optical fibre made from glass.

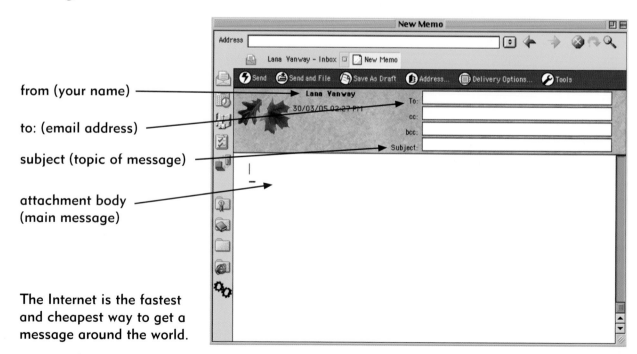

from (your name)

to: (email address)

subject (topic of message)

attachment body
(main message)

The Internet is the fastest and cheapest way to get a message around the world.

How does the Internet work?

The Internet uses a special system called a 'packet switched system protocol'. This means it sends information in small packets. If a communication line is cut or broken, the packet finds another path through the network of computers. Most people access the Internet by subscribing to a company called an Internet service provider (ISP). An ISP offers public access to the Internet through distribution technologies such as phone, cable or satellite.

1. A person writes an email message on their personal computer using email software.

2. The personal computer logs onto the **server** of the Internet service provider using the telephone line.

3. The person sends the email to the server over the telephone line.

4. The person that the email is addressed to logs onto the server.

5. The server **downloads** a copy of the email to the receiver's address.

What's next?

In the future, wireless connections will make connecting to telephone lines optional. Users will be able to connect directly to the ISP server by radio. This will free people from having to access the Internet from specific fixed points. The main phone-line system, however, will continue to carry most of the Internet traffic.

Websites

A website is a location on the World Wide Web. Each website contains a home page on a topic, which users see when they enter the site. The site might also contain additional documents, files or web pages and links to other websites.

Where used?

Anyone with access to the Internet can visit a website or build their own website. People can log onto websites from computers in homes, cafes and offices.

How used?

A website is stored on a central computer linked to the Internet. People who want to visit the website type the web address into a computer program called a web browser. When they don't know the address, they can use a search engine to find the site.

Materials

Information on a website is made up of digital text, **graphics**, audio and video files, and hyperlinks to other web pages. Websites can range in size from as little as one page to a vast number of pages. Websites are designed to take up minimum computer space, so computers logging onto them can quickly open each page.

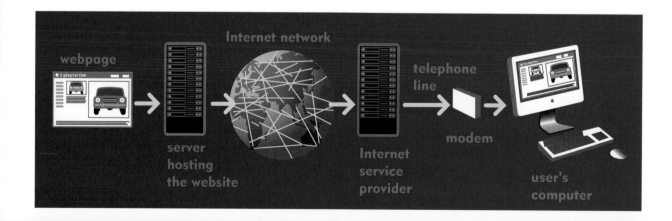

How do websites work?

A website is a collection of web pages, each page being a document saved in Hyper Text Markup Language (HTML). The pages are stored on a main computer called a web server. People use computer programs called web browsers to log onto a web server. They can then view web pages by downloading them on to their computer. The information presented on web pages can range from very simple text, to visual delights that use film, animation and sound.

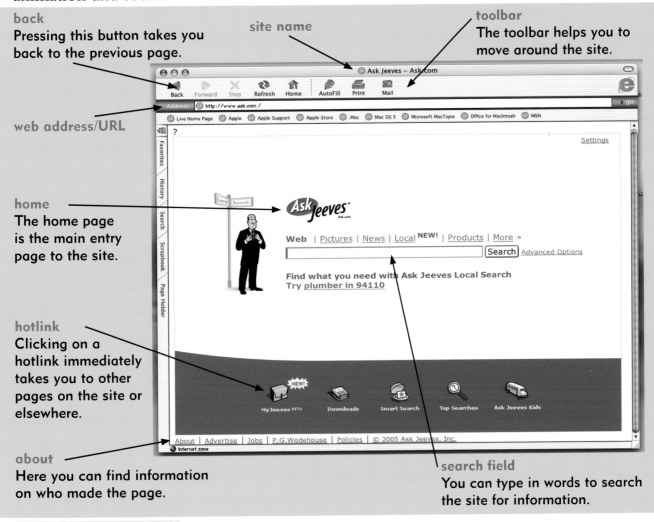

back
Pressing this button takes you back to the previous page.

site name

toolbar
The toolbar helps you to move around the site.

web address/URL

home
The home page is the main entry page to the site.

hotlink
Clicking on a hotlink immediately takes you to other pages on the site or elsewhere.

about
Here you can find information on who made the page.

search field
You can type in words to search the site for information.

What's next?

In the future, websites will automatically deliver summaries of new content to a 'newsreader' on your computer desktop.

How well does it work?

In this book you have read about and looked at the designs of many different technologies. As well as understanding how technology works, we also need to think about how well it works in relation to other needs, such as aesthetic, environmental and social needs. We can judge how well the idea, product or process works by considering questions such as:

Manufacture	• Is the manufacture of the technology efficient in its use of energy and resources?
Usability	• Does the technology do the job it is designed to do? • Is it safe to use? • Is it easy to use?
Social impact	• Does it have any negative effects on people?
Environmental impact	• Does using the technology have any environmental effects? • Does it create noise, cause pollution or create any waste products?
Aesthetics	• Does the design fit into its surroundings and look attractive?

Thinking about these sorts of questions can help people to invent improved ways of doing things.

This man is trialling a new electronic tourist guide which includes a global positioning system, an Internet link to travel information and weather reports, and a language translator.

Glossary

alloys mixtures of metals

cable thick bundle of electrical wires that are bound together and insulated

circuits paths along which an electrical current or signal can be carried

circuitry a system of electrical circuits

digital information stored in the form of numbers, called binary code

downloads copies a file from a central Internet server

electromagnetic a combination of waves of electric and magnetic fields carrying energy from one place to another—light, heat, microwaves, X-rays and radio waves are all different wavelengths of electromagnetic radiation

exchange a facility where lines from telephones are linked together to enable communication

graphics anything displayed on a computer screen that is not text

liquid crystal a device that displays images by the action of electrical signals on a grid of liquid cells

magnet metal that can pull iron or steel objects towards it and hold or move them

mains electricity electricity that is provided by a power company that generates and distributes electric energy

microprocessor the central processing unit (CPU) or silicon-chip 'brain' of a computer

network a group of connected computers that can communicate with one another

orbit the path taken by an object in space as it revolves around another object

program a set of instructions for a computer to carry out

receivers devices that detect radio signals and convert them into sound

satellite a machine placed in orbit around Earth to perform a job, such as relaying communications signals

server a central computer which stores Internet files for people on the network to access

silicon a substance found in sand, clay and many minerals, and used in computer chips, alloys, and building materials

silicon chip a wafer-thin slice of silicon, smaller than a finger nail, which contains thousands of microscopic electronic circuits

solar panels large, flat panels that change sunlight into electricity.

transmission transfer of a signal, message, or other type of information from one location to another

transmitters parts of radio systems that transmit, or send, radio signals

Index